THE STORY OF ESTHER

Activity Book for Beginners

The Story of Esther Activity Book for Beginners

Bible Pathway Adventures® is a trademark of BPA Publishing Ltd.

ISBN: 978-1-9992275-0-0

Author: Pip Reid

Creative Director: Curtis Reid

For free Bible resources including coloring pages, worksheets, puzzles and more, visit our website at:

www.biblepathwayadventures.com

 # Introduction for Parents

Enjoy teaching your children about the Bible with our *Esther Activity Book for Beginners*. Packed with detailed lesson plans, coloring pages, worksheets, crafts and puzzles to help educators just like you teach children a Biblical faith. Includes scripture references for easy Bible verse look-up and a handy answer key for teachers.

Bible Pathway Adventures helps educators teach children a Biblical faith in a fun and creative way. We do this via our Activity Books and free printable activities – available on our website: www.biblepathwayadventures.com

Thanks for buying this Activity Book and supporting our ministry. Every book purchased helps us continue our work providing free Classroom Packs and discipleship resources to missions and families around the world.

The search for Truth is more fun than Tradition!

★BONUS★

The Chosen Bride storybook is available for download.
Type the link into your browser to get your FREE copy today!
https://BookHip.com/GJHAXL

Table of Contents

LESSON 1 | Lesson Plan
Party at the palace

Teacher: _____

Today's Bible passage: Esther 2:8-14

Welcome prayer:
Pray a simple prayer with the children before you begin the lesson.

Lesson objectives:
In this lesson, children will learn:
1. Why the king sent the queen away from the palace
2. Why Esther came to Susa

Did You Know?
The king's second party lasted for seven days.

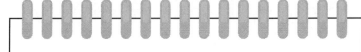

Bible lesson overview:
King Ahasuerus was the king of Persia. He was a rich and powerful king. In the third year of his reign, he held two parties at his palace in the city of Susa. During the second party, he asked Queen Vashti to come and see him. The queen disobeyed him and said, "No." This made the king angry. He talked with his Wise Men and decided to send her away forever. Now he needed a new queen! Soon, many girls began arriving in Susa. They wanted to marry the king. Among them was a Hebrew girl named Hadassah. But everyone called her Esther. Esther's cousin Mordecai told her, "Do not tell anyone you are a Hebrew or who I am."

Let's Review:

Questions to ask your students:

1. Who ruled the kingdom of Persia?
2. Who was the queen?
3. Why did the king send the queen away?
4. Who was Esther's cousin?
5. What was Esther's secret?

A memory verse to help children remember God's Word:

"Esther didn't tell anyone she was a Hebrew." (Esther 2:10)

Activities:

Worksheet: Trace the Words

Coloring page: Party at the palace

Worksheet: What do you eat at a party?

Worksheet: My party meal

Worksheet: G is for gold

Connect the dots: King of Persia

Labyrinth: The palace

Bible word search: The palace

Puzzle: What is Esther's secret?

Closing prayer:

End the lesson with a small prayer.

❧ Trace the Words ❧

Color the pictures.

Party at the palace

The king held a party for seven days.
Draw the king and his guests at the party.

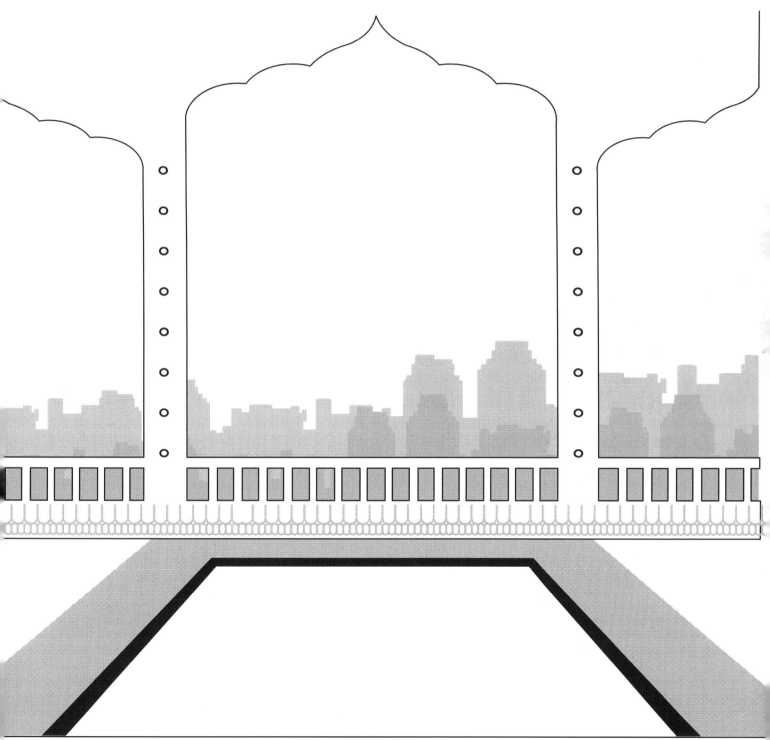

What do you eat at a party?

Color the food you eat red.

bread

cookie

ice cream

sandwich

cake

meat

pancakes

My Party Meal

What food do you eat at a party?
Draw the food you like to eat.

🌿 G is for Gold 🌿

At the party, people drank out of cups made from gold.
Trace the letters. Color the picture.

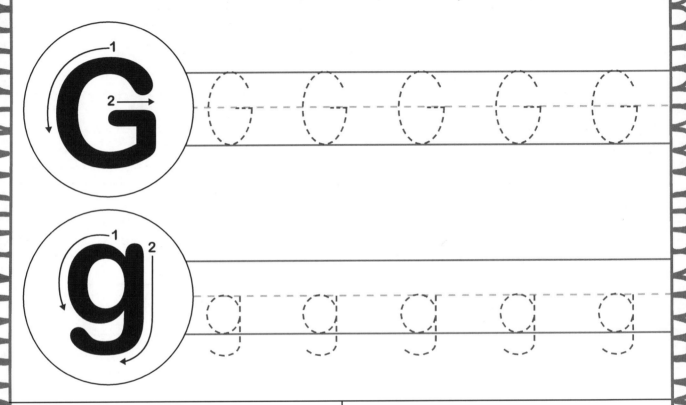

Trace the letter g

Color the gold

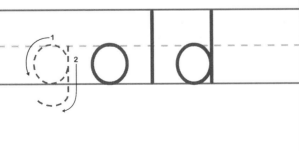

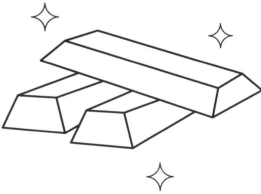

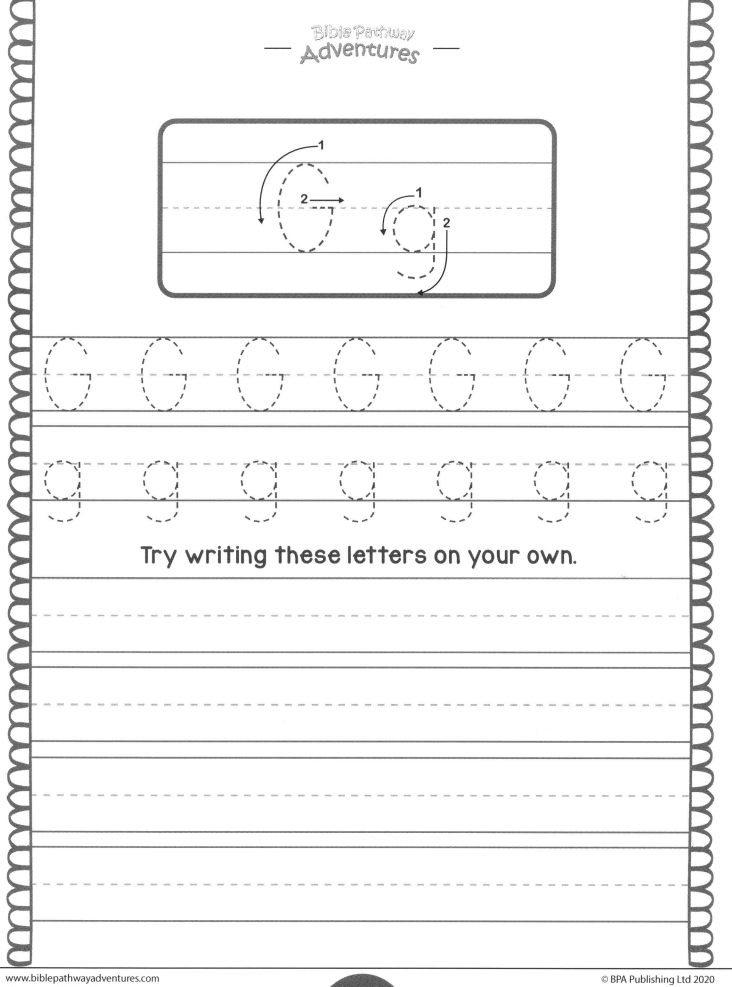

Try writing these letters on your own.

King of Persia

The king of Persia held a party at the palace.
Connect the dots to see the picture.

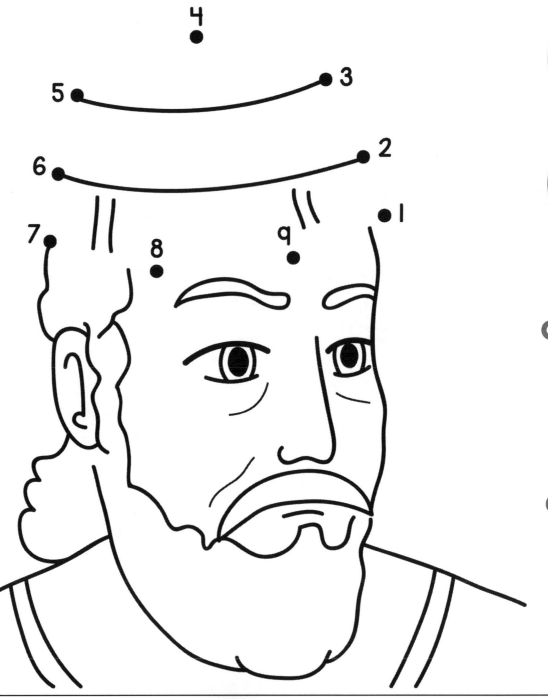

The Palace

Help Esther find the palace.

✿ The palace ✿

Find and circle each of the words from the list below.

K I N G P Q
F O O D A U
R O B B R E
A Y X Y T E
G I R L Y N
G O L D P U

PARTY   QUEEN
KING   GOLD
FOOD   GIRL

What is Esther's secret?

Fill in the blanks using the chart below. What do you see?

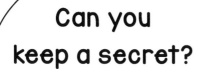

Can you keep a secret?

$\overline{5}$ $\overline{19}$ $\overline{20}$ $\overline{8}$ $\overline{5}$ $\overline{18}$

$\overline{9}$ $\overline{19}$ $\overline{1}$

$\overline{8}$ $\overline{5}$ $\overline{2}$ $\overline{18}$ $\overline{5}$ $\overline{23}$

A	B	C	D	E	F	G	H	I	J	K	L	M
1	2	3	4	5	6	7	8	9	10	11	12	13

N	O	P	Q	R	S	T	U	V	W	X	Y	Z
14	15	16	17	18	19	20	21	22	23	24	25	26

LESSON 2 | Lesson Plan
Esther marries the king

Teacher: _____

Today's Bible passage: Esther 2:12-18

Welcome prayer:
Pray a simple prayer with the children before you begin the lesson.

Lesson objectives:
In this lesson, children will learn:
1. How Esther prepared to meet the king
2. Who the king chose to be the new queen

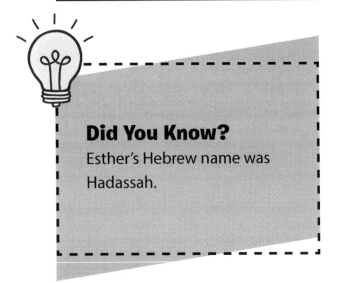

Did You Know?
Esther's Hebrew name was Hadassah.

Bible lesson overview:
For one year, Esther and the girls got ready to meet the king. They were given beauty treatments with oils, spices, and perfumes. Esther had seven servants just to help her get ready! After twelve months, Esther went to see the king at his royal palace. The king loved Esther more than all the other girls. He put a crown on her head and made her the new queen. He threw Esther a big party and sent gifts to the people because he was a generous king.

Let's Review:

Questions to ask your students:

1. How long did Esther prepare to meet the king?
2. How did Esther prepare to meet the king?
3. Do you think Esther was nervous to meet the king?
4. Why did the king marry Esther?
5. What did the king send people after he married Esther?

 A memory verse to help children remember God's Word:

"The king….made Esther the new queen.." (Esther 2:17)

 Activities:

Worksheet: P is for Palace
Worksheet: The number seven
Worksheet: Esther gets ready
Worksheet: Tracing map
Esther Flashcards
Coloring page: Esther meets the king
Coloring page: A new queen
Worksheet: I spy!
Coloring activity: The king's gift
Bible craft: Make a crown
Worksheet: Matching pairs
Worksheet: The happy king

 Closing prayer:

End the lesson with a small prayer.

P is for palace

The king of Persia lived in a palace.
Trace the letters. Color the picture.

P is for palace

The number seven

Seven women helped Esther get ready to meet the king.
Write the number seven. Color the perfume bottles.

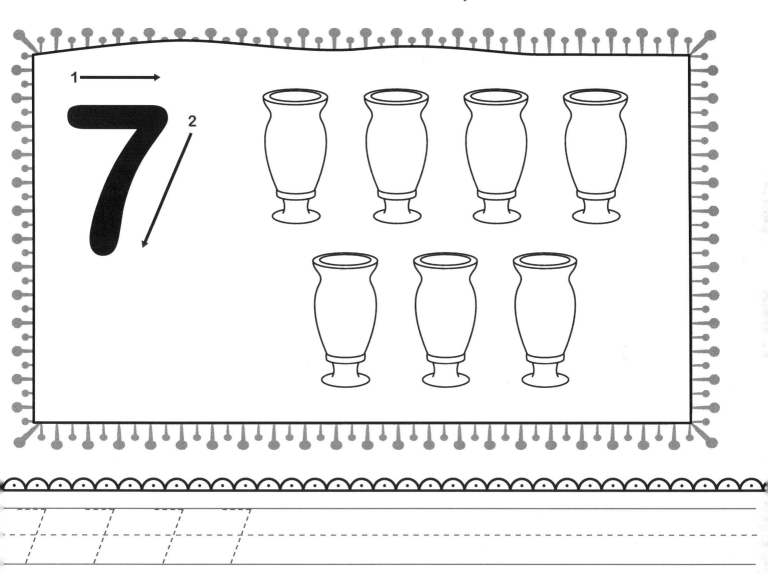

🌿 Esther gets ready 🌿

Esther used perfume and special oil to get ready
to meet the king. Draw a circle around the pots and jars.
Use a red crayon to fill them with oil and perfume.

Esther meets the king

Trace along the line to help Esther find
the palace and meet the king.

 Esther meets the king

Draw Esther and the king to complete the picture.

The new queen

The king loved Esther more than the other girls.
He made her the queen. Trace the words.
Color the picture.

Queen Esther

🌿 I spy! 🌿

Esther visited the king at the palace. Color the same object a single color. Then count each type of object and write the number on the label.

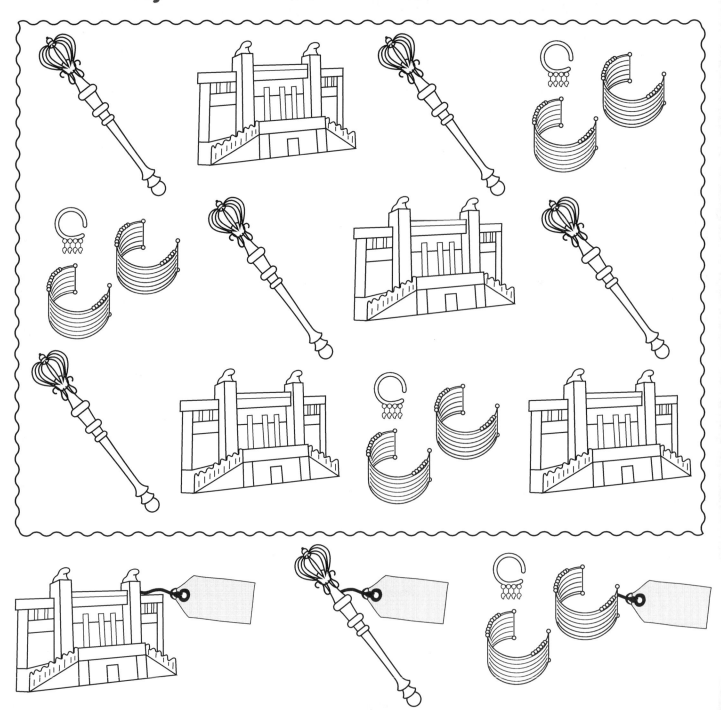

🍃 The king's gift 🍃

The king sent gifts to the people to show he was happy.
A gift is something given to a person on a special day
like a birthday or wedding. What did the king give
the people? Use your imagination to draw a gift!

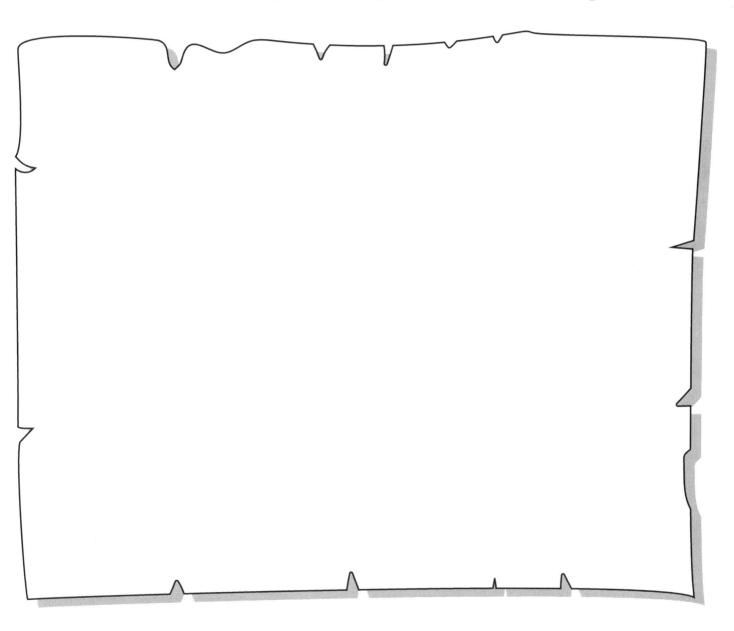

Matching pairs

Draw a line between the matching objects.
Color the matching objects the same way.

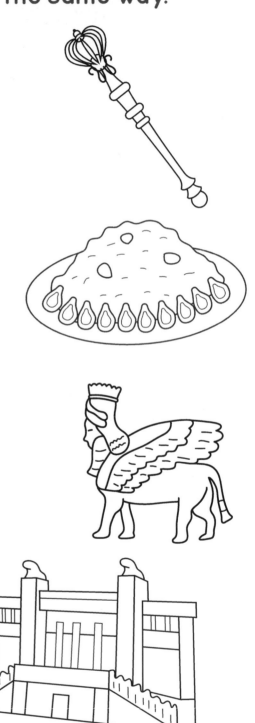

The happy king

The king loved Esther more than the other girls.
He was happy to make her the new queen.
Circle and color the happy faces.

LESSON 3 | **Lesson Plan**
The wise queen

Teacher: _____

Today's Bible passage: Esther 4:12-5:5

Welcome prayer:
Pray a simple prayer with the children before you begin the lesson.

Lesson objectives:
In this lesson, children will learn:
1. Who had an evil plan to destroy the Hebrew people
2. How Esther prepared to meet the king

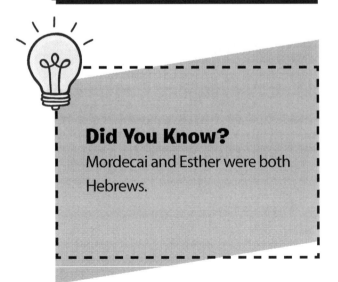

Did You Know?
Mordecai and Esther were both Hebrews.

Bible lesson overview:
At this time, there lived a wicked man named Haman. One day, he told the king about a group of people (Hebrews) who did not obey the law. He had a plan to stop them! The king agreed with Haman's plan. "Do what you want with them," he said. The king wrote letters to people in his kingdom telling them about the plan. When Mordecai heard about the plan, he asked Esther to ask the king to change his mind. Esther prayed and did not eat for three days. Then she went to see the king. The king was happy to see Esther. He showed her his rod of gold and said, "I will give you anything you ask for." Esther said, "I have prepared a meal (feast) for you and Haman. Come to the meal."

Let's Review:

Questions to ask your students:

1. Who had an evil plan to get rid of the Hebrews?
2. Did the king agree with the evil plan?
3. How did Esther prepare to meet the king?
4. Was the king happy to see Esther?
5. What did Esther tell the king?

A memory verse to help children remember God's Word:

"Maybe you live in the kingdom for a time like this." (Esther 4:14)

Activities:

Coloring page: Haman

Worksheet: The king's ring

Map activity: The Persian Empire

Bible activity: The palace

Bible activity: I can write!

Worksheet: R is for rod

What's my sound? R

Worksheet: The number three

Worksheet: Esther was brave!

Worksheet: E is for Esther

Closing prayer:

End the lesson with a small prayer.

🌿 Haman 🌿

Haman did not like the Hebrews. Trace the word.
Color the picture.

Haman

☙ The king's ring ☙

The king wore a special ring on one of his fingers.
He gave this ring to Haman to show he liked Haman's plan.
Draw a ring on one finger. Count the fingers.

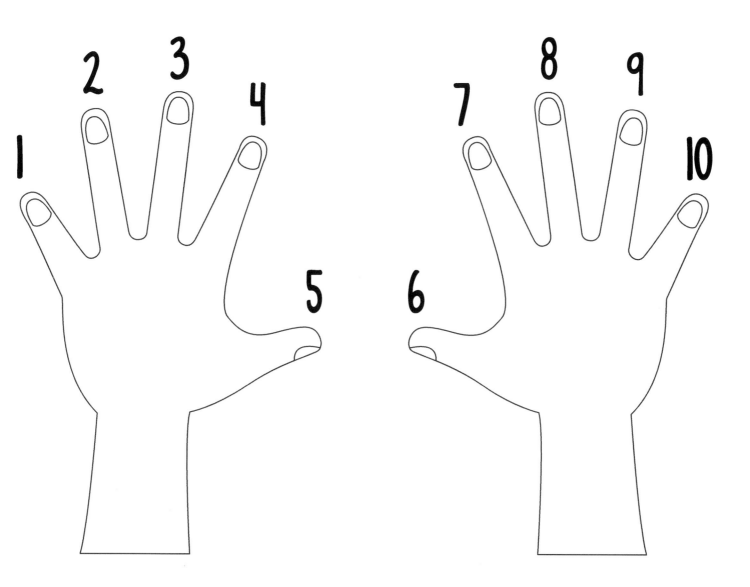

🌿 The Persian Empire 🌿

The king sent letters to the people in his kingdom.
Connect the dots to see where the letters were sent.
Color the map.

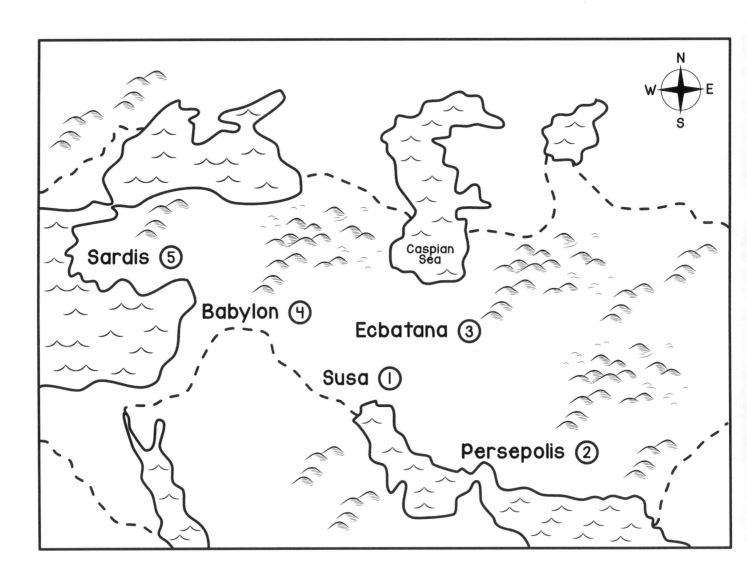

🌿 I can write! 🌿

When Esther was alive, people wrote on clay tablets.
Write on your own clay tablet. Trace the word.

tablet

✦ R is for rod ✦

The king's rod was made of gold. Trace the letters.
Color the picture.

r is for rod

🌿 What's my sound? 🌿

The word 'rod' starts with the letter R.
Circle and color the pictures that have the
same beginning sound as rod.

ram

lion

rocket

cow

raft

The number three

Esther did not eat or drink for three days.
Then she went to see the king at the palace.
Write the number 3. Color the pictures.

🍃 Esther was brave! 🍃

Being brave is doing the right thing even when it is hard.
Esther was brave to go and see the king.
Think about a time you were brave.
Draw yourself doing something brave below.

E is for Esther

Esther asked the king to come to a party (Esther 5:4).
Trace the letters. Color the picture.

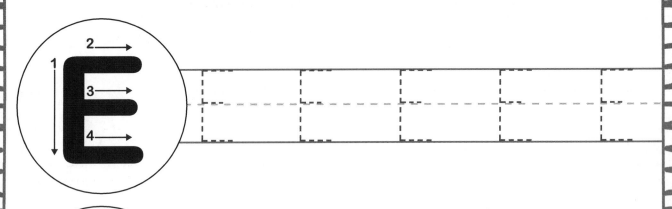

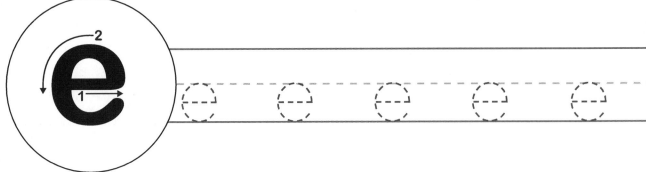

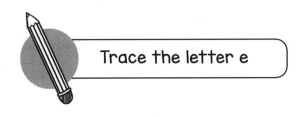

Trace the letter e

Color the picture of Esther

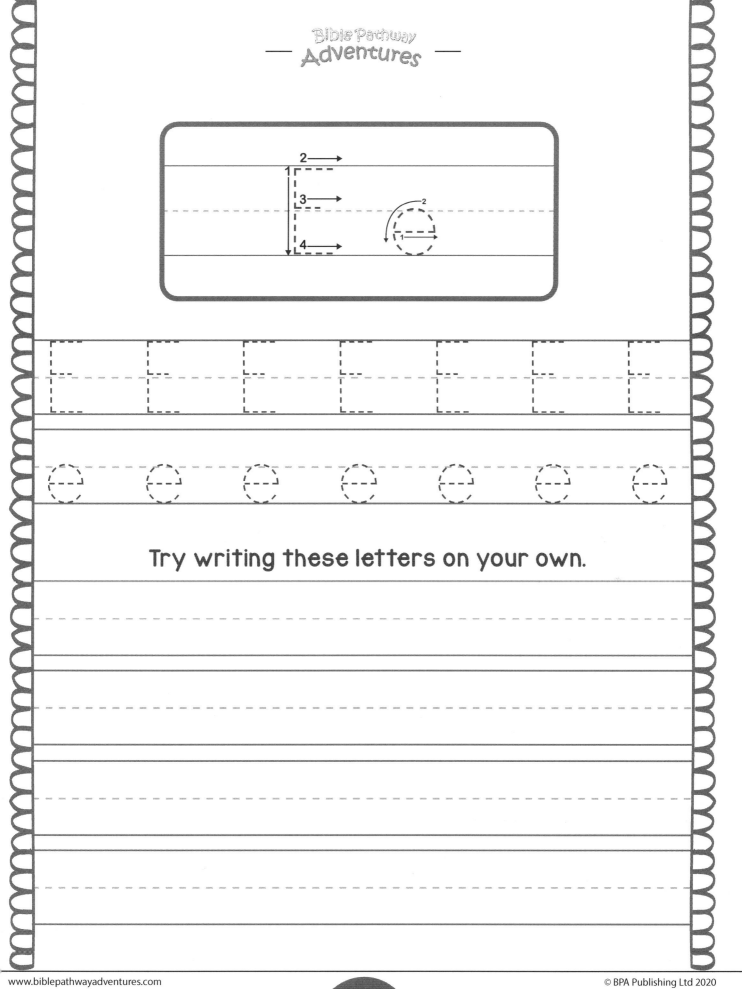

Try writing these letters on your own.

LESSON 4 | Lesson Plan
Mordecai's reward

Teacher: _____

Today's Bible passage: Esther 6:1-11

Welcome prayer:
Pray a simple prayer with the children before you begin the lesson.

Lesson objectives:
In this lesson, children will learn:
1. How Mordecai saved the king's life
2. How the king rewarded Mordecai

Did You Know?
Mordecai rode through the city streets on one of the king's own horses.

Bible lesson overview:
After the meal (feast) with Esther and Haman, the king could not sleep. He asked his servants to read him a story about the kingdom. As the king listened, he learned that many years ago, a brave man named Mordecai had saved his life. The king wanted to reward Mordecai. So when the wicked Haman came to see him, the king asked, "How shall I reward a man?" Haman puffed out his chest. He thought the king was talking about himself. But the king wanted to reward Mordecai instead. He told Haman to dress Mordecai in special clothes and take him on horseback through the city streets.

Let's Review:

Questions to ask your students:

1. Why did the servants read to the king?
2. Who saved the king's life many years ago?
3. Who did the king want to reward?
4. What animal did Mordecai ride on?
5. Who took Mordecai through the streets?

 A memory verse to help children remember God's Word:

"This is done for the man the king wants to reward." (Esther 6:11)

 ## Activities:

Connect the dots: Mordecai

Worksheet: M is for Mordecai

Bible craft: Esther necklace

Worksheet: Trace the words

Coloring page: Mordecai's reward

Bible word search: Mordecai's reward

Bible activity: The king's robe

Worksheet: Follow the path from A-Z

Worksheet: What's different?

 ## Closing prayer:

End the lesson with a small prayer.

Mordecai

Mordecai helped save the king's life.
Connect the dots to see the picture.

Mordecai

Let's learn about the letter M.

Mm Mm Mm Mm Mm

Mordecai   Mordecai

Circle each M

T	b	M	u	G
m	V	c	j	e
R	M	f	s	m

Bible Pathway Adventures

Trace the Words

Color the pictures.

esther

rod

tablet

crown

 Mordecai's reward

Mordecai rode on a horse through the city streets.
Draw Mordecai on the horse.

🌿 Mordecai's reward 🌿

Find and circle each of the words from the list below.

```
M E N Y R C
G L K J O I
B E Q F B T
B O O K E Y
H O R S E Q
K I N G O E
```

MEN   BOOK
KING   HORSE
CITY   ROBE

 The king's robe

The king gave Mordecai a robe to wear.
Design and color a robe for Mordecai. Use your imagination!

Follow the path from A-Z

Help Mordecai make his way through the city by following the path from A to Z.

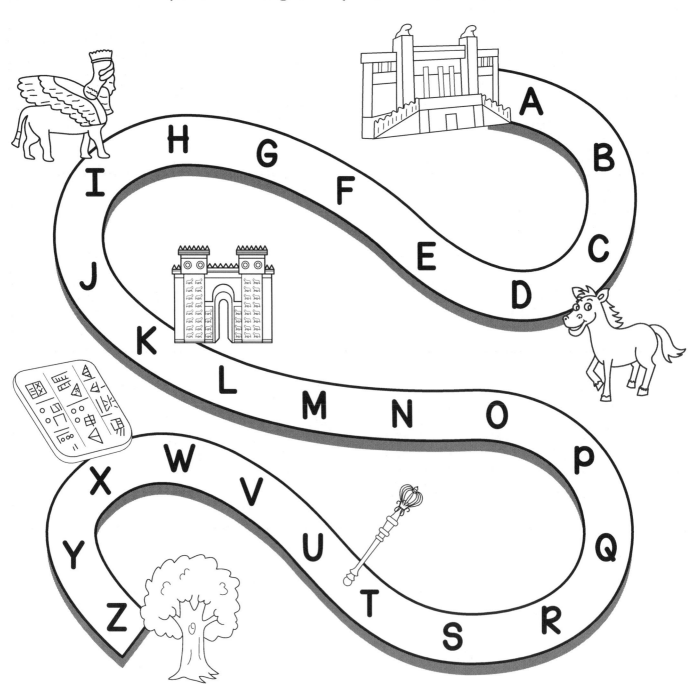

🌿 What's different? 🌿

Circle the picture that is different.

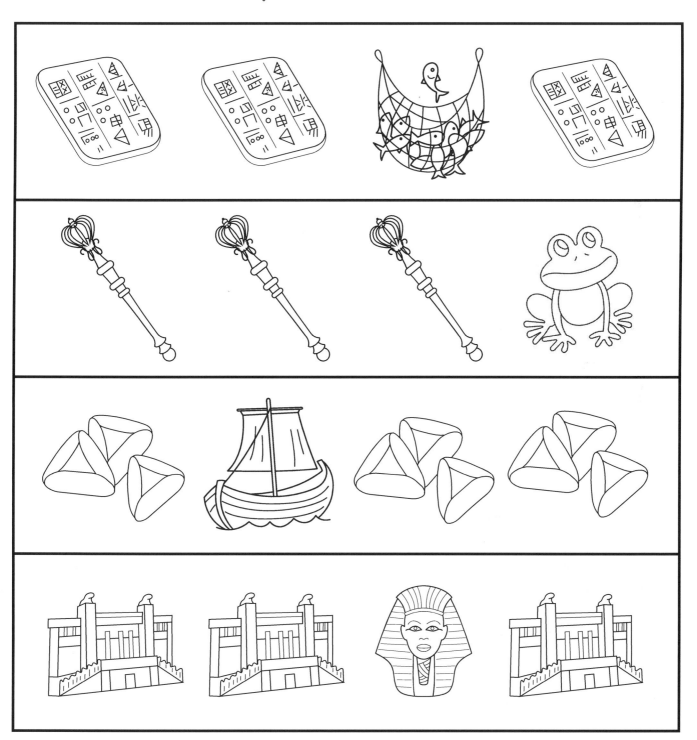

LESSON 5 | Lesson Plan
Esther saves her people

Teacher: _____

Today's Bible passage: Esther 8:11-17

 Welcome prayer:
Pray a simple prayer with the children before you begin the lesson.

Lesson objectives:
In this lesson, children will learn:
1. How the king learned about Haman's evil plan
2. How Esther helped saved the Hebrews

Did You Know?
Purim is the name of the holiday that remembers how Esther saved the Hebrews.

Bible lesson overview:
Haman and the king ate another meal with Esther. There, Esther told the king about Haman's plan to destroy the Hebrews. Haman was in big trouble! The king told his servants to hang Mordecai on a post. Esther spoke to the king again. She asked him to save the Hebrews. And the king did so. He made a new law giving the Hebrews permission to stop their enemies from hurting them. Men riding fast horses took letters to people everywhere in the kingdom. The letters told everyone about the king's new law. The Hebrews were happy! Esther had helped save her people.

Let's Review:
Questions to ask your students:
1. Who ate a meal with Esther?
2. What did Esther ask the king?
3. How did the king save the Hebrews?
4. What did the king's letters say?
5. What is the name of the day that remembers how Esther saved the Hebrews?

 A memory verse to help children remember God's Word:
"It was a happy day for the Hebrews." (Esther 8:16)

 Activities:
Bible activity: The feast
Memory verse coloring: Esther
Worksheet: The messengers
Worksheet: H is for horse
Worksheet: Matching pairs
Let's learn Hebrew: Ester
Worksheet: Counting practice
Counting activity: Hamantaschen
Let's Draw: Draw a gift
Craft: Gift tags
Worksheet: True or False?
Certificate of Award

 Closing prayer:
End the lesson with a small prayer.

"Perhaps you have come to the kingdom for such a time as this."

(Esther 4:14)

The messengers

Help the messengers take letters to the people by coloring the letter m.

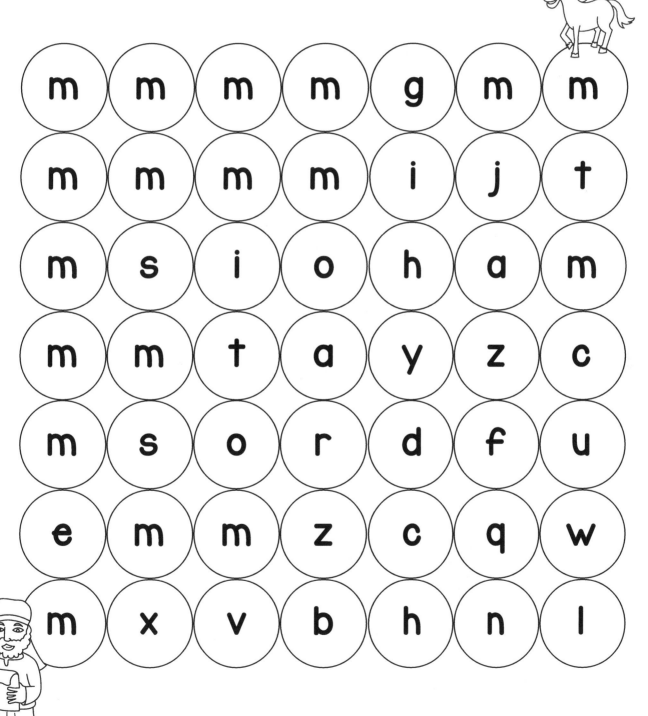

m	m	m	m	g	m	m
m	m	m	m	i	j	t
m	s	i	o	h	a	m
m	m	t	a	y	z	c
m	s	o	r	d	f	u
e	m	m	z	c	q	w
m	x	v	b	h	n	l

✷ H is for Horse ✷

is for

horse

🌿 Matching pairs 🌿

Draw a line between the matching objects.
Color the matching objects the same way.

✫ Ester ✫

The Hebrew name for Esther is Ester.
Esther went to the king and asked him to save the
Hebrew people. Esther was very brave!

Ester

אֶסְתֵּר

Esther

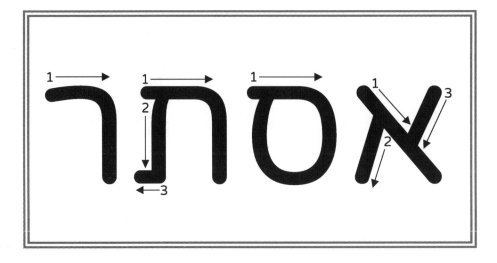

 Let's write! ✏️

Write the Hebrew word 'Ester' on the lines below.

אסתר

אסתר

Try this on your own.
Remember that Hebrew is read from RIGHT to LEFT.

Counting practice

Color the square with the correct number of objects in each box.

Esther

2
5
3

Rod

1
5
4

Purim

6
3
4

Tablet

3
6
1

🌿 Hamantaschen 🌿

What a lot of Hamantaschen!
Can you count them and write the number?

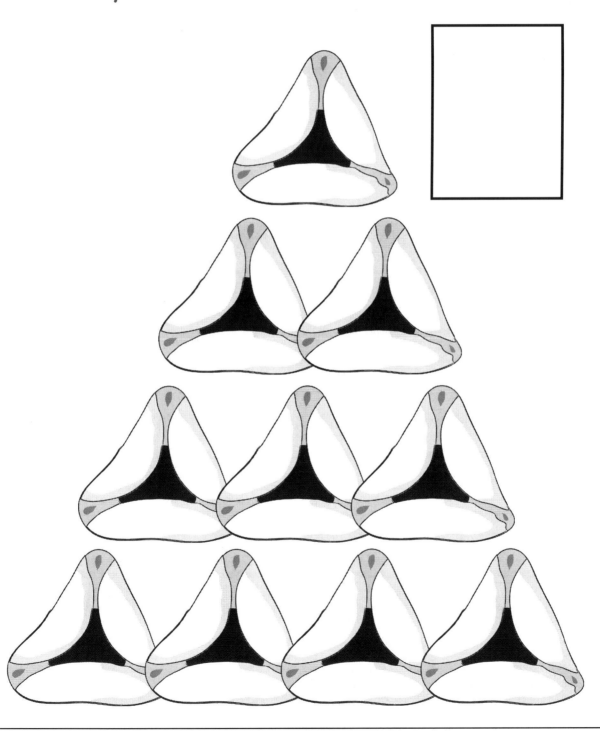

Let's Draw

People celebrate the festival of Purim by giving
gifts to each other. Draw a gift for someone in your family.

✿ True or False? ✿

Listen to the statements. Are they true or false?

Esther was
a Hebrew.

Mordecai was
a fireman.

Mordecai rode
a horse.

Esther did not eat
for one month.

The king did not
like Esther.

Esther was
the queen
of Persia.

CRAFTS & PROJECTS

❧ Make a crown ❧

You will need:
1. Heavy card stock
2. Paint, felt pens, or crayons
3. Scissors (adult only)
4. Extra-strength glue sticks or tape

Instructions:

1. Paste the crown template onto heavy card stock. Color and cut out the crown and long rectangle strips.
2. Ask your child to decorate their crown.
3. When they have finished decorating the crown, glue the long rectangle to the sides of the crown.
4. Wrap the crown around your child's head. Fasten the rectangle strips together using a glue stick or tape.

ta-da!

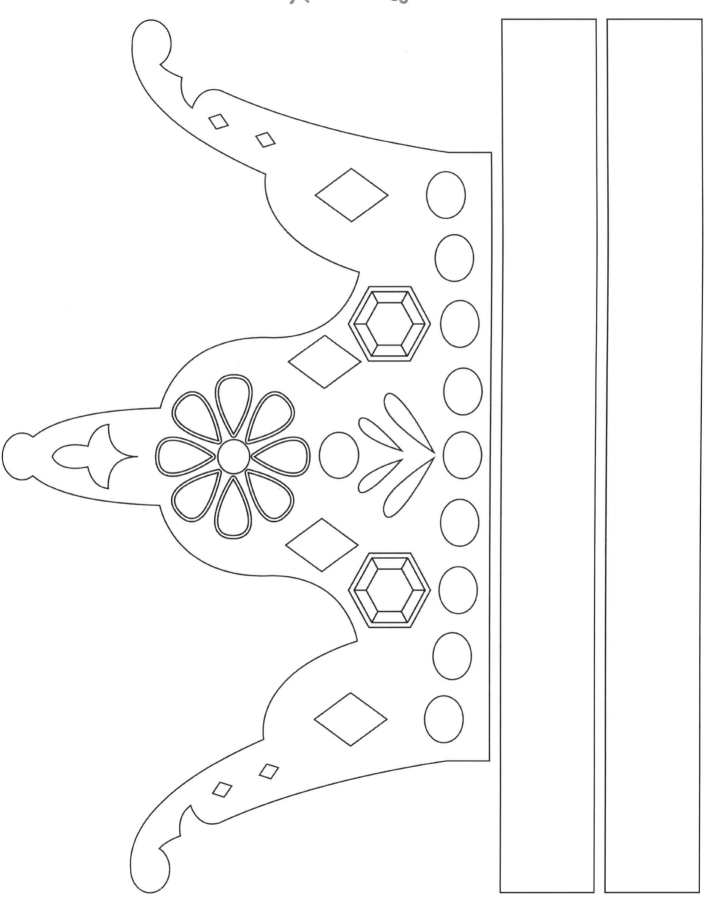

✂ Flashcards ✂

Color and cut out the flashcards.
Tape them around your home or classroom!

king

5

queen

6

crown

7

jar

8

🌿 The palace 🌿

The king lived in a royal palace. Color and cut out the people.
Place them in the palace.

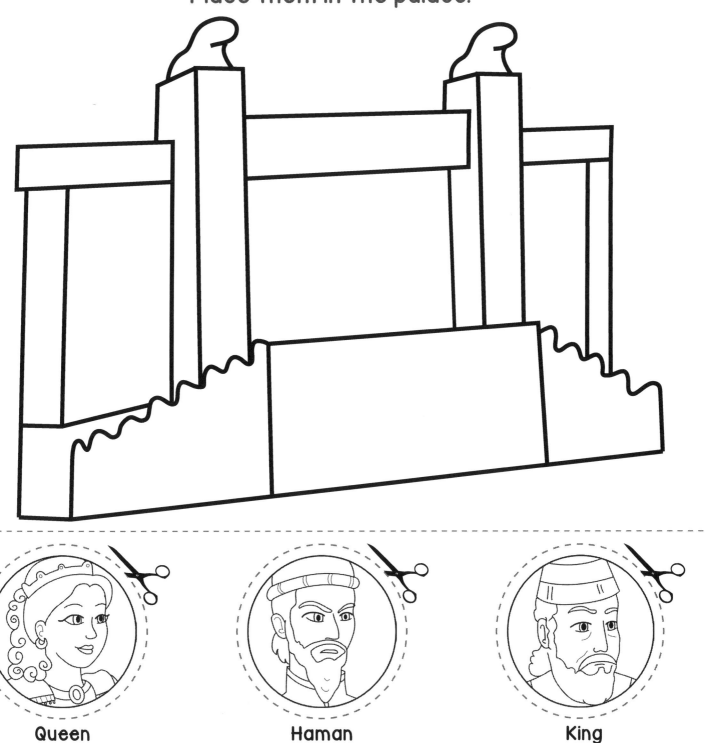

Queen

Haman

King

🌿 Craft: Esther necklace 🌿

You will need:
1. Esther pictures (see next page)
2. Paint, felt pens, or crayons
3. Scissors or hole punch
4. Yarn or string

Instructions:

1. Have your children color the pictures from the story of Esther.
2. Cut out the pictures (children may need to help with this step).
3. Use a hole punch or scissors to create a hole in each of the circles.
4. String the circles with yarn or string to create an Esther necklace.

1.   2.   3.   4.

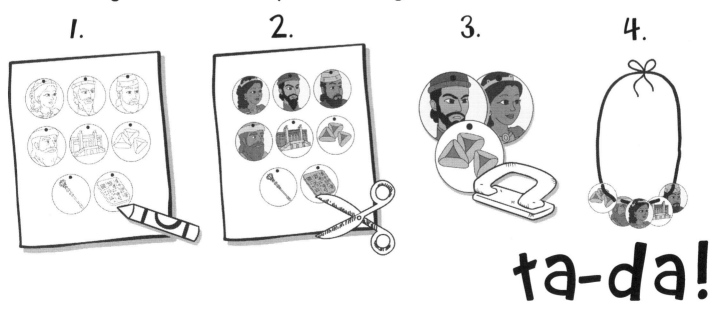

ta-da!

❧ The feast ❧

Esther invited two men to a feast. Who were they?
Color and cut out the people. Place them around the table.

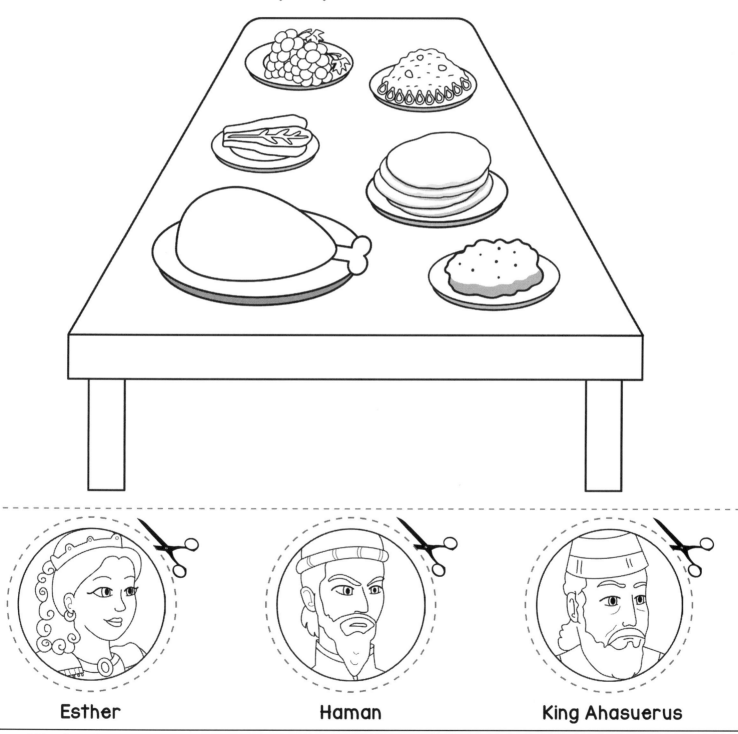

Esther

Haman

King Ahasuerus

Craft: Gift tags

You will need:
1. Gift tag template (see next page)
2. Scissors (adults only)
3. Crayons or pencils

Instructions:

1. Help your child to color and cut out the Hamantaschen gift tags.
2. On the back of each gift tag, have your child draw a picture or write their name.

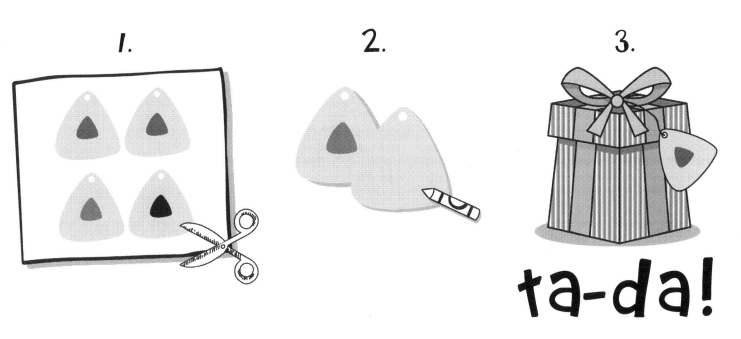

1.   2.   3.

ta-da!

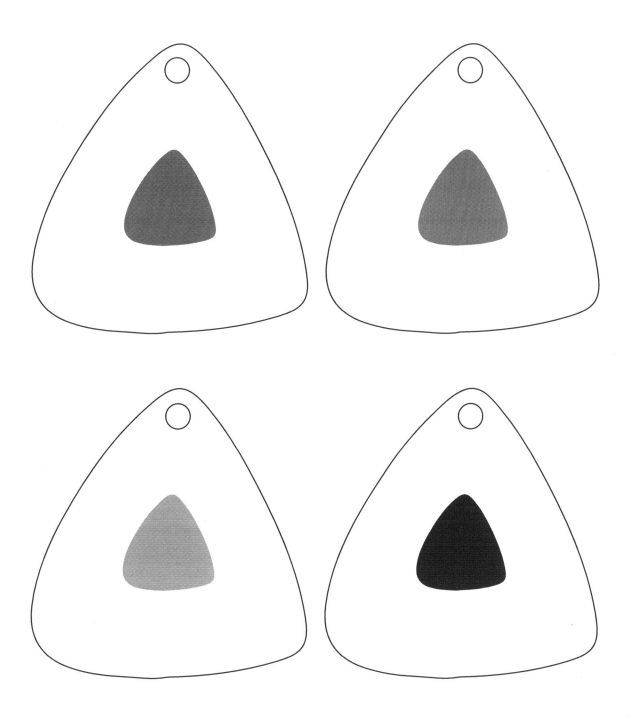

Certificate of Award

Certificate of Award

Congratulations

For

Signed

ANSWER KEY

LESSON ONE: Party at the palace
Let's Review answers:
1. The king
2. Queen Vashti
3. Because she disobeyed him
4. Mordecai
5. She was a Hebrew

LESSON TWO: Esther marries the king
Let's Review answers:
1. One year
2. With special oils, spices, and perfumes
3. Prompt children to answer this question
4. The king loved Esther more than the other girls
5. The king sent people gifts

LESSON THREE: The wise queen
Let's Review answers:
1. Haman
2. Yes
3. She fasted and prayed for three days
4. Yes he was
5. Esther invited Haman and the king to a meal (feast)

LESSON FOUR: Mordecai's reward
Let's Review answers:
1. The king could not sleep
2. Mordecai
3. Mordecai
4. A horse
5. Haman

LESSON FIVE: Esther saves her people
Let's Review answers:
1. Haman and the king
2. To save the Hebrews
3. He made a new law, giving the Hebrews permission to defend themselves from their enemies
4. The Hebrews are allowed to defend themselves from their enemies
5. Purim

True or False?
Answers:
Esther was a Hebrew. (True)
Mordecai was a fireman. (False)
Mordecai rode a horse. (True)
Esther did not eat for one month. (False)
The king did not like Esther. (False)
Esther was the queen of Persia. (True)

Discover more Activity Books!

Available for purchase at www.biblepathwayadventures.com

INSTANT DOWNLOAD!

The story of Esther	Paul's Shipwreck
The Exodus	Moses Ten Plagues
Jonah and the Big Fish	Birth of The King
Noah's Ark	Esther

Made in the USA
Coppell, TX
24 July 2022